Dreams Bedtime Stories

Bedtime Stories for Kids Great Selection of story about Friendship, Modern Fairy Tales and Relaxing Sleep Tales.

By Robert Santos

© Copyright 2021 by - All rights reserved.

This document is geared towards providing exact and reliable information regarding the topic and issue covered. The publication is sold with the idea that the publisher is not required to render accounting, officially permitted, or otherwise qualified services. If advice is necessary, legal or professional, a practiced individual in the profession should be ordered.

From a Declaration of Principles which was accepted and approved equally by a Committee of the American Bar Association and a Committee of Publishers and Associations.

In no way is it legal to reproduce, duplicate, or transmit any part of this document in either electronic means or in printed format. Recording of this publication is strictly prohibited and any storage of this document is not allowed unless with written permission from the publisher. All rights reserved.

The information provided herein is stated to be truthful and consistent, in that any liability, in terms of inattention or otherwise, by any usage or abuse of any policies, processes, or Instructions contained within is the solitary and utter responsibility of the recipient reader. Under no circumstances will any legal responsibility or blame be held against the publisher for any reparation, damages, or monetary loss due to the information herein, either directly or indirectly.

Respective authors own all copyrights not held by the publisher.

The information herein is offered for informational purposes solely and is universal as so. The presentation of the information is without contract or any type of guarantee assurance.

The trademarks that are used are without any consent and the publication of the trademark is without permission or backing by the trademark owner. All trademarks and brands within this book are for clarifying purposes only and are the owned by the owners themselves s, not affiliated with this document.

Table of content

Chapter 1: Fairy tales for kids to read at bedtime 4

1.1. A tale of two young sisters.. 4

1.2. The Naughty Boy 11

1.3. A not so liked doll 14

1.4. The match girl... 18

1.5. The Shadow... 22

Chapter 2: Bed Time Fictional Stories 43

2.1 The Covetous Aristocrats... 43

2.2 Rebecca of Toronto.. 46

2.3 The Dress-Maker and the Three Behemoths..................... 50

2.4 The Fortress of Luck.. 58

Chapter 1: Fairy tales for kids to read at bedtime

An example of a folk genre that takes the shape of a short story is a fairy tale, fairy tale, wonder tale, magic tale, or Märchen. Traditionally, these tales involve creatures such as dwarfs, dragons, angels, fairies, giants, gnomes, goblins, griffins, mermaids, singing birds, trolls, unicorns or witches and generally spells or enchantments. There is no straight line in most cultures that distinguishes legend from folk or fairy tale; both of these combined form the literature of preliterate societies. Fairy tales can be distinguished from other folk stories such as legends (which typically involve belief in the veracity of the described events and explicit moral tales including fables of the beasts).

1.1. A tale of two young sisters

In a faraway empire there lived 2 girls, Rosie and Daisy. The older sibling was Daisy, and the younger Rosie. They had lived in a château. They were concept princesses. Daisy was very meek and selfish. She loved hurting everyone including her sister, but Daisy was really kind to her father as she believed that in the future her father, the king, would hand over her the kingdom. Rosie was really loving, affectionate and friendly. She'd never made complaints to her dad.

One day the King decided for his daughters to divide the empire into two equal halves. The king asked Daisy, "Daisy, what do you like the most about the whole world? "If she expressed pearls or jewels, Daisy thought her father might be disappointed and give Rosie the whole kingdom. She lied instead, "Papa, of course it's you! "She smiled when it was Rosie's turn, and said," Oh! Daddy, I do want millions of things. But the best ones are rain, rainbow, smiling babies, helping others and watching people smile. "The king's face turned red with anger. He disciplined Rosie by telling her to quit the country for a week.

Rosie has always left the castle sad. When she heard someone sobbing she started walking out. It was a tree made of coconut. Rosie inquired why the sobbing took place. The tree replied that in a couple of days none of them had watered it, and so it could die. Rosie said "My mate, don't worry. I'm going to help you. "There was a lake nearby and she dug a narrow canal from the lake to the tree, so the coconut tree could constantly be watered. The coconut tree was so pleased and he thanked her. Rosie waved the tree and had her journey resumed. She saw a weeping cow and a weeping calf. She went to them, and settled them down. The calf screamed "My mum hasn't had a hay for several days, if it goes on she won't be able to feed me. I 'm going to be starved to death. There's no Master here. He would have fed my mum if he had been here. "Rosie reassured the calf not to worry. She went on her quest for hay and grass. She came back with a large bundle of hay. This was more than enough, until the owner came back. Rosie grinned and rode happily forward, after being thanked by the mother cow and the calf. She heard the crying of tiny voices and sought them out. It took her some time to realize they had come down from below. It was ants crying. She asked about them. In between the cries the ants shouted. They said "There was a heavy downpour and it sprinkled our anthill." Rosie felt sad and got an idea. She said "I will go gather some mud and help you create a better area of your ant hill." Rosie succeeded in the challenge. The ants hopped with happiness, and thanked her.

She reached a woodland as she walked farther along. She saw a hut in the distance. She was so tired of walking and helping others; she wanted to rest and knocked that way at the door. An elderly woman opened the door. Rosie asked if she could have anything to eat and take some rest. In turn, she'd do all the housework. The old woman had been inviting her in. She provided some food for Rosie to eat. Rosie didn't tell the old woman she was a princess because she didn't want to treat the old lady like one. Rosie stayed in the hut for a week, and did all the work. The next day, Rosie told the old woman that she had to leave. Whether she might get a shampoo and soap she told the old lady. The old woman gave them a dress she asked for along with it. The old woman gave a package to Rosie, and told her to open it in her room only. Rosie started his way back to the castle. She'd worked with the bees. They delivered her diamonds and stones. The master of the cow and calf had returned on her return journey and gave Rosie milk, sweets and dairy goods, and the master had asked some people to take the milk to Rosie's home. She ended up meeting the coconut tree and it gave her a few coconuts. Whispered the coconut tree, "These are particular coconuts. Wait in your place, and just open them.

Rosie made it to the castle. She knelt down at the threshold. The king unlocked the way to see a girl in surprise. He asked: "Who's that? "Rosie was amazed.

She responded: "Papa! Your aunt is me, Rosie. "The king did not believe his eyes. He asked Rosie, "How did you get so pretty, and how did you grow your hair so long? "Didn't Rosie know she was pretty? She glanced in the mirror and went. She had indeed glowed with magnificence.

Rosie hopped excitedly and pleaded with her father, "Let's go to my room and open those gifts." She was astonished at the jewelry, which shone like the sun. She pulled one out, and lo! A new one superseded the old one. She turned from the coconut tree towards the gift. They looked like regular coconuts but gold coins spilled out when she opened them. As Rosie proceeded to take the coins she kept re-filling again and again. Rosie asked her dad to give everybody in the kingdom the jewels and the coins. Daisy truly was jealous. She told her father that she would study in another kingdom but had other ambitions. She went to the spot where Rosie had gone.

She found the coconut tree. The coconut tree begged Daisy to water him. Daisy shouted pompously: "Never! If I water you, my dress will get dirty. "Saying this she went on and met the cow and the calf, who begged her to give them some hay. Daisy responded promptly in a negative tone "No! If I give you some hay, my hands and dress will become dirty. "She said this, kicked them and started walking away. She had seen the ants needing aid in constructing their ant-hill. Daisy replied pessimistically, again, "No! I'm allergic to mud and bugs. "She hurried off. She finally attained the house of the old woman. She exclaimed, "Old Lady, I am the princess of a country, and I have come to honor you by staying in your house for a week." The old woman responded, "Please stay in my house and help me with the cooking and other items." And I'm a princess. That is not what I am doing. You do the other tasks and the cooking. I will never do anything like that in a filthy house like this. "The old lady cooked and washed.

A week passed. Daisy announced, "Before I go back to my kingdom, I need the best soap, shampoo, and dress with beautiful sequins." Patiently, the old woman got her all she wanted. Daisy asked the old woman to give Rosie more of her gifts than she gave. The gifts were donated by the old woman. Daisy started walking away with no thanks.

She had met the ants as she began to walk back to her castle. The army of ants started biting her legs and face. Everywhere she had started to swell. She escaped. She met the cow and the calf, who began kicking her the way she kicked them. And next was the coconut tree. It started tossing coconuts over Daisy's hands. Her head hurt with little bumps and began to swell. She asked, "Don't hurt me please," and she ran away.

She was close to the castle and wasn't able to contain any more suspense and wanted to open her present. So she was greeted at the bottom when she opened it, by a swarm of bees and weeds. She threw away the box, and ran to the chateau. She knocked on the door of the castle and the King emerged. Daisy shouted, "Daddy, it's me, Daisy," and the king said, "It can never be! It's not my Daisy that is. The king said, "That can never be! This is not my Daisy. My Daisy has long hair and wears a beautiful dress." Daisy was astonished by the King's statement and touched her own head but she was bald. She shouted "No!"

Daisy told the king she was still worrying Rosie and explained to the king in detail what happened when she visited the old woman's house to reassure her dad that she would never hurt someone and that she would no longer be angry. She learned her lesson and after that she always lived happily.

Help Ever, Hurt Never, the moral of the story.

1.2. The Naughty Boy

A thoroughly kind old poet, lived a long time ago. One night he was sitting. In his room there arose a terrible storm outside, and rain flowed from the sky. In his chimney, where the fire and the roasting apple burned, the poet sat nice and cozy.

Hissed.-Hissed. "They're not going to wet up to the skin those who have no ceiling over their heads," the good old poet said. "Oh, let me in! Let me in! Let me go in! Let me in! I'm cold, I'm wet! I'm wet! "Suddenly a kid exclaimed who was weeping at the door, calling for admission as the rain fell, and the wind fell all the way.

"Wretched thing! 'The old poet said as he opened the door. A little boy stood there, very nude, and the water poured down from his long golden hair; he began to shake with fear, and if he had not found a warm room, he would surely have drowned in the terrifying rain. "Poor babe!" The old poet said, taking the boy by the hand. "Come in, get in and I will reestablish you soon! You're going to have wine and roasted apples, because you're a lovely child! "And the boy truly was. His eyes were like 2 bright stars; and while his hair was filtered down by the water, it waved in beautiful curls. He looked almost like an angel, except he was so weak, and his entire body was shivering with cold. He had a lovely little bow in his hand but the rain was pretty ruined, and the shades of his other-colored arrows ran into each other. Sitting next to his side, the old poet took the little fellow on his lap; he pressed the water out of his soaking head, warmed his hands between his own, and made some good wine for him. Then the boy managed to recover, his cheeks grew rosy again, he jumped from the lap where he was sitting, and started dancing around the old, kind poet.

"You are a merry fellow," said the old man. "What's your name?" "My name is Cupid," answered the boy. "Don't you know me? There lies my bow; it shoots well, I can assure you! Look, the weather is now clearing up, and the moon is shining clear again through the window." "Why, your bow is quite spoiled," said the old poet. "That were sad indeed," said the boy, and he took the bow in his hand and examined it on every side.

"Oh, it's clear again, and it doesn't hurt at all; the cord is really tight. I'm going to try it directly. "And he twisted his bow, aimed, and shot an arrow right into his heart at the old poet. "You see now that there was no spoil in my bow," he said laughing; and he ran away. The naughty boy, that way to shoot the old poet; the one who took him to his warm room, who treated him so graciously, and who gave him warm wine and the best apples! The unfortunate poet was lying on earth and crying, because the arrow had really went into his head.

"Fie!" He said. "What a nasty Cupid guy! I would warn all the children of him, that they may be wary and not play with him, for he will only bring them anguish and heartbreak for years. "And all the precious kids to whom he told this story took great care of this wicked Cupid; but he always called them fools, for he is remarkably crafty. When the university students return from the lessons, he races in a long jacket alongside them, and with a book underneath his belt. It is quite difficult for them to know him, so they move arm in arm with him, as if he, too, were like themselves a learner; and then, silently, he thwacks an arrow to their buttocks. When the young ladies come to be analyzed by the priest, or go to church to be verified, he's close behind them again. Yes, he continues to follow people forever. He lies in the large chandelier at the play and burns in dazzling sparks and folks assume it's a true blaze, but they soon learn it's something different. He roams in the palace orchard and on the walls: yes, he even fired your parent's right in the heart. Only ask them and you'll hear what they'll tell you. Oh, that Cupid is a silly child; you should never have anything to do with him. He is running after everybody forever. Only think, he shot your senile grandma with an arrow once! But that's a good while ago, and now it's all past; though, she never forgets a thing of that kind. Fie, cupid idiot! But you know him now and you also know how ill he behaves!

1.3. A not so liked doll

Susie sat on the supermarket shelf, her body covered with a layer of dust. She felt like crying as she observed that all the other toys were going home. She had long been in the store and everybody had forgotten about her. Once upon a time Susie was a beautiful rag doll, with bright yellow hair yarn and big blue eyes. Her once beautiful blue dress was in dire need of washing. She longed to go home with a special little girl and be loved and admired but when they came to the shop, nobody even smiled at her. That was because she lost an arm and no one even tried to stitch that back together. Her arm sat for a very long time alongside her on the shelf day and night, just sitting there waiting to be put back on her. But none have ever done so.

It was the most magical moment of the year, Christmas once again. All the toys in the store flew off the shelves to go out to loving kids and warm, cozy homes. All but Susie. She was already sitting there accumulating ashes, her arm resting on the shelf beside her. It has reminded her how unloved she was all the time.

She had so desperately wanted to cry. No one will ever bring her around. She was doomed to sit for the rest of her doll-life on that shelf, and be sad and lonely. She watched as the pink little elephant descended from the shelf. She watched the little brown puppy dog step away from the table. She watched the tall, fuzzy green frog step away from the table. All the other dolls also had gone off the shelf.

Still, she was left there, one more time. Christmas Eve arrived and it was still early in the day. Susie always sat on the shelf and looked sadder than ever before. She would never, a little girl would ever love him. She would always and forever sit on that shelf.

The door-bell tinkled and she saw a pretty young woman and a little girl walked in. The little girl had a cast on her right leg and was in a wheelchair.

"Good morning," said the handsome young woman to the shopkeeper.

"Good morning," answered Mr. Gray, staring over his spectacles at them. "What can I make of you?"

"This is my cute little girl Nicole," she introduced. "She had met an accident. She fell down while she was ice skating and hurt her leg thereby breaking it. She knows that Santa is coming tonight to bring her presents but I promised her that she could pick out something nice for herself. She wants a doll. Do you have any here?" He shook his head. "I'm afraid not. All my dolls have been sold for the holiday."

"Mum, look! "When the little girl pointed at her, Susie's heart climbed into her chest.

"Behold the doll. She looks so lonely sitting by herself there." "That doll you don't want, "Mr. Brown told her. "She's old and covered in dust and she misses her arm. It requires to be stitched back on. I don't know why I always have her there, to tell you the truth. A long time ago, I would have put her in the trash." "No, "the little girl wept. "She too needs love! "Can we see her," asked the charming, young lady. Scowled Mr. Dark. "Good yourself, love." He went and got Susie off the shelf and gave her to the little kid, lacking arm and all. The small girl hugged her close to her. "Mama, please may I have her? She's a pretty doll. She's just broken like I am now." "I suppose we could clean her up. And it wouldn't be a problem to sew that arm back on." She looked at the shop keeper asking: "How much is this for, sir?" "Well," Mr. Brown scratched his chin with his nails thoughtfully, "I suppose you could have her for free, since she was going to end up in the garbage anyway."

"But I have to give you something for her," insisted the mother, as she opened her bag. The shop keeper looked at the little girl, who hugged Susie. She almost seemed happy with the old dusty doll and knew the little girl was going to clean her up and have her look pretty in no time. "To me, the smile on the face of your little girl is enough compensation." He bent down and look at Nicole. "You're going to be looking after her, won't you? "She was laughing at him. "I promise! Oh yes! So I love her! She just wants a bit of affection and I'm going to give her it! Let's head home now, sweetheart! "And Susie never felt happier as the little girl cuddled her close to her. For the once undesirable doll it was the most happy and joyful Christmas ever!

1.4. The match girl

It was terribly cold; it was snowing and almost black, and it was evening — the last night of that year. In this cold and gloom a little girl walked down the lane, bareheaded and with foots bare. She had slippers on when she left home, it is true; but what was the good of it? They were very large slippers that had been worn by her mother up to now; they were so big; and they were lost by the poor little girl when she scuffled up the street because of two carriages that rolled by incredibly quickly. One slipper was not found anywhere; the other was picked up by an urchin and took off. For it; he figured he'd do it for a cradle because he was supposed to have a day even the girls. So the little girl walked on with her tiny naked feet, red and red. Blue and cold. In an old apron, she brought a lot of matches and kept a packet of them in his side. Nobody bought anything from her throughout the whole day; nobody gave her a single. Farthing ...... farthing. With cold and hunger, she crawled along trembling — a very picture of sorrow, a sad little thing! Snow-flakes covered her long fair hair, which fell round her neck in beautiful curls; but of course she never talked of that once. The candles were gleaming from all the walls, and it smelled like roast goose so deliciously, because you know it was New Year's Eve; yeah, she thought of it. She sat in a corner formed by two homes, one of which was more advanced than the other. Down, and they cowered. She had drawn her little feet close to her but she grew colder and colder. Hot, she didn't move to go anywhere, because she hadn't sold matches and couldn't hold a fire. Money farthing: she would certainly get blows from her father and it was also cold at home, because she had just the roof over her, from which the breeze whistled, even though the largest gaps were stopped with rags and straw.

Her palms were almost frozen with cold. Oh, oh! A match could give her a world of ease, if she only dared to take one from the bag, place it against the wall and rub her fingers by it. She pulled an out. "Rish!" How blazed it was, how burned it was! As she placed her hands over it, it was a soft, bright flame, like a candle: it was a wonderful fire. It really seemed as if the little maiden was sitting in front of a large iron stove, with lustrous brass feet on top and a brass ornament. With this blessed influence the fire burned; it warmed so pleasingly. The little girl had already reached out her feet to fire them up too; but — the little flame went out, the heater vanished: she had in her hand just the remains of the burnt-out match. She rubbed another against the stone: it burned brilliantly, and the stone was translucent as a shield when the light shone on the wall, so that she could see into the house. A snow-white tablecloth was spread over the table; on it was a splendid porcelain service, and with its fillings of apple and dried proms, the roast goose steamed notably. And what was even more capital to behold, the goose hopped down from the platter, rumbled on the floor with a knife and a fork in her breast, until it reached the poor little girl; when — the game went out and nothing but the thick, cold, waterlogged girl

It had left the wall behind. She brightened up another play. Now she was sitting there under the most beautiful Christmas tree: it was much bigger and more adorned than the one she had seen in the wealthy merchant's house through the glass windows.

They are now as stars in heaven; one fell down and formed a long trail of fire. "Someone is just dead!" said the little girl; for her old grandmother, the only person who had loved her, and who was now no more, had told her, that when a star falls, a soul ascends to God. She drew another match against the wall: it was again light, and in the luster there stood the old grandmother, so bright and radiant, so mild, and with such an expression of love. "Grandmother!" cried the little one. "Oh, take me with you! You go away when the match burns out; you vanish like the warm stove, like the delicious roast goose, and like the magnificent Christmas tree!" And she rubbed the whole bundle of matches quickly against the wall, for she wanted to be quite sure of keeping her grandmother near her. And the matches gave such a brilliant light that it was brighter than at noon-day: never formerly had the grandmother been so beautiful and so tall. She took the

Thousands of lights shone on the green trees, and gaily-colored images stared down upon her, as she had seen in the store windows. When the match went out the little girl held out her hands toward them. The Christmas tree's lights soared higher and higher, she saw little maiden on her back, and both flew so high, so very high in glory and happiness, and then there was neither ice, nor hunger, nor fear above — they were with God. But the little girl stood in the corner, at the chilly hour of dawn, with rosy cheeks and a smiling smile leaned against the wall—frozen to death on the last evening of the old year. Stiff and strong sat the child with her matches, one bundle of which had been burned. "She wanted to get hot on herself," said folks. No one had the slightest idea of what wonderful things she had seen; nobody really fantasized of the magnificence with which she had stepped into the pleasures of a new year with her grandmother.

1.5. The Shadow

It is the sun rising in the dry fields, sure enough! The citizens there are quite a mahogany black, yea, and they are burned to Negroes in the HOTTEST fields. Yet now it's for the HOT only lands that a learned man came from the cold; he thought he could run around just as much but soon he discovered his mistake when at home.

He and all sensible people were forced to stay in the doors, the window shutters and the doors. The entire day closed; it seemed like the entire house was asleep, or there was nobody at home. The narrow street with the high houses has been designed so that the morning sunlight has to disappear. It was really not to be borne till evening. The wise man from the frozen lands-he was a young man and seemed to be a smart guy-was sitting in a sparkling oven; it had an effect on him, it was pretty meagre — even his shadow shrunk in, ... Sun had an impact on it too. It was at night when the sun was down that they started refresh. Again window has a balcony in the warm lands, and the people came out on all of the balconies in the street — one must have air, even if one is used to being mahogany! * Both were lively and straight down the street. Tailors, shoemakers, and all the residents went out to the streets. And tables were brought forth — and candles were burned — yes, there were more than a thousand lights burning. The one spoke and the other sang; and people walked and the bells of the church rang, and the asses walked. A dingle-dingle-dong with it! Because they had bells on too. The market boys yelled and hissed,

And screaming and firing, with devils and balls detonating — and the bearers of the body came and hood carriers — for there were psalm and hymn funerals

— and then the carriage driving and company arriving: yes, in truth it was quite lively down the street. It is just in this particular room, standing opposite to that in which the learned stranger lived, was still; and yet someone lived there, for the balcony had flowers — they grew so well in the heat of the sun! And that they couldn't do it unless they were watered — and somebody had to water them—here's anyone. The opposite door was also opened late at night but it was dark inside, at least in the front room; the sound of the music was heard further in.

He thought it was pretty amazing, but now — maybe he just dreamed it — he noticed it all wonderful out there, in the warm lands, if only there was no sun. The odd landlord said that he didn't know who took the opposite room, one didn't see somebody and the other guy.

Art, it was incredibly tiresome to him. "It's like someone was out there, learning a part he couldn't master — still the same part. 'I'll be master of it! 'Says he, but somehow he can't learn that, however long he's running.

* In Danish, the term mahogany can be translated as having two meanings. Overall it says: The reddish-

brown wood itself, but in jest it says "excessively fine." Nyboder's anecdote, in Copenhagen (the seamen's quarter) A sailor's aunt, who has always been a sailor. She came to her neighbour, proud and perfect, and complained that she had a splinter in her. Right. "What, then? "Asked the wife of a neighbor. "This is a splinter in the mahogany," the other said. "And Mahogany! Couldn't be happier like you! "The lady exclaimed—and from there the proverb, 'It's so. Mahogany! "It is extracted-(that is, extremely fine). One night the stranger woke up — he slept with the balcony doors open — the curtain before it was lifted by the breeze, and he felt a peculiar luster came from the house of the opposite neighbour; all the flowers shone like fire, in the most exquisite colors, and a tall, elegant maiden stood in the middle of the flowers — it was as if she shone too; the light always hurt his eyes. He now opened them wide — yes, he was very awake; he was on the floor with one spring; he crawled softly behind the curtain, but the maiden was gone; the flowers didn't shine any more, but they remained there, new and blooming as ever; the door was adjar, and the music sounded quiet and lovely, that one might almost melt away from it in sweet thoughts. Yet it was like an enchanting object.

And who has lived in it? Where was the actual admission? The entire ground floor was a row of shops, and it was not always possible for people to run through. The man sat out on the balcony one evening. The light burned in the room behind him; and so it was quite natural for his shadow to fall on the wall of his opposite neighbour. Hey! There it stood behind the flowers on the railing, immediately opposite; and as the stranger passed, the shadow always passed: for that it still did. "I think my shadow is the only living thing you can see over there," the educated man said. "See how perfectly it lies between the flowers. The door is half-open: the shadow should be cunning now, and it should go into the room, look around, and then come and tell me what it had seen. Here, here on now! Be useful, and do a service to me," he said, in jest. "And the graciousness to walk in. Now it's time! Aren't you? "And then the shadow nodded, and the shadow nodded once more. "Well then, come on! But don't get away with it. The random man rose, and his shadow also went up on the balcony of the opposite neighbour; the stranger turned round and the shadow turned round as well. Yeah! If anyone had paid special attention to it, they would have seen, quite distinctly, that the shadow had gone through their opposite neighbor's half-open balcony-door, just as the random person had gone into his own room, and let the long curtain fall behind him. The educated guy went out the next morning to drink coffee, and read the newspapers. "What is it? "When he came out in the sunshine, he said. "I don't own a shadow! So, it simply went out last night, and did not come back again. It is absolutely exhausted! "This irritated him: not so much because the shadow had passed out, but because he knew there was a legend of a man without a shadow. * That was clear to all at home, in the cold lands; so if the learned man now came there and told his story, they would say that he imitated that, and that he had no reason to do so. Therefore he wouldn't think about it at all; and that was considered wisely. * Shadow less Man, Peter Schlemihl. He went out on the balcony again during the evening. He had put the light directly behind him, because he realized that for a screen, the shadow would always have its master, but he could not attract him. He made himself small; he made himself great; but no shadow returned. He'd say, "Ah! Yeah, hey! "But it was useless. It was vexatious; but everything grows so rapidly in the warm lands; and after a delay of eight days, to his great joy, he observed that a new shadow was coming in the sun. He had a rather good shadow over the course of three weeks, which grew more and more on the road as he set off for his home in the northern lands, so that at last it was so long and so big, that it was more than enough. Then the wise man came home and wrote books on what was real in the world, and on what was good and what was beautiful; and days and years passed — yea! She passed away several years. One evening there was a gentle knocking at the door, as he was sitting in his bed. "Hop in! "And he said, but no one came in; and he opened the door, and there stood before him a man so exceedingly lean, that he felt very strange. As for the others, the guy was dressed very fine — he must be a gentleman. "Whom do I have the honor? "The learned guy asked." Yes! I thought so much,' the fine man said. "I thought you didn't know me. I have a lot of muscle. I got clothes and flesh even. You definitely never imagined that you could see me so well off. You know your old shadow, don't you? Of sure you thought I would never come here again. Ever since I was last with you, things have gone well with me. I have been very well off in all respects. Should I buy my service free? If so, I can do it; "and then he rattled a whole bunch of valuable seals hanging from his watch, and stuck his hand in the thick gold chain he was wearing around his neck — nay! How his fingers glittered with the rings of diamonds; and then they were all pure gems. "No; I can't recover from this shock! "The learned man said," What is all this meaning? "It's not something common," the shadow said. "But you do not belong to the social order yourself; and I, as you well know, have followed in your footsteps from a boy. I went my own way as soon as you realized out I was tired of moving out in the world alone. I'm in the brightest circumstances, but a kind of desire came over me to see you again before you die; you're going to die, I guess? I wanted to see this land again too — because you know we really miss our ancestral country. I know you've got another shadow again; do I or you have anything to give about it? If so, you'll pressure me to tell you what it is. "Nay, you really are? "The educated man said, 'it's quite remarkable: I never thought that one's old shadow will come back as a man.' 'Ask me what I've got to pay,' the shadow said, 'and I don't like being in some sort of debt.' 'Why do you speak about that? "What liability is there to talk about?" the learned man asked. Make yourself as free as anyone else would. I am pleased to learn of your good fortune: sit down, old buddy, and inform me a little how it went with you, and what you saw in the warm lands of our opposite neighbor." "Yes, I'll tell you all about it, "said the ghost, and sat down," but then you must also assure me that, when you meet me, you'll never tell anyone here in the city that I was yours. I 'm going to get betrothed, so I will provide for more than one child." "Be at peace with that, "said the educated one;" I'm not going to say anybody who you really are: here's my hand — I swear it, and a man's bond is his name." "A name is a shadow, "said the shadow," and as such it must speak. "It was really very incredible how much a guy it was. It was dressed entirely in black, and of the finest cloth; it had patent leather shoes, and a hat that could be folded together, so that it was a bare crown and brim; not to speak of what we already know it had — seals, gold neck chains, and rings of diamonds; yes, the shadow was well-dressed, and that's just what made it a man. "Now I'll tell you my adventures," said the shadow; now maybe that was out of arrogance; because the shadow on the ground kept so still and silent that it could hear everything that was going on: it needed to see how it could free itself and make its way up to becoming its own lord. "Oh, who lived in the house of our opposite neighbour? The shadow said. "It was the loveliest of all beings, it was Poesy! I've been there for three weeks, and that has the same impact as if you've existed for three thousand years, absorbing all that's been written and composed; that's what I'm doing, because it's true. I have done it all and I know it all! "Poetry! "The wise man screamed." Yes, yes, she still dwells in vast cities as a recluse! Poetic! Yes, I saw her — a single brief moment, but sleep came in my eyes! She was standing on the balcony, shining as Aurora Borealis shines. Go on, go on — you wert on the balcony and went through the gate, and then—"I was then in the antechamber, "the shadow said. "You always sat in front of the antechamber, looking over. There was no light; there was a kind of twilight, but through a long row of rooms and lounges the one door was opened directly opposite the other, and there it was lighted up. If I had gone over to the woman, I would have been absolutely killed; but I was circumspect, I took the time to consider, and that one must always do. "The educated man asked. "I saw it all, and I'm going to tell you all of it: but — it's no privilege on my part — as a free man, and with the understanding I have, not to talk of my situation in life, of my excellent circumstances — I definitely wish you would tell me YOU *! "* In Denmark, it is the practice of intimate friends to use the single second voice, 'Du,' (thou) when referring to one another. When a friendship is formed between men, they usually endorse it, when occasion offers to each other, either in public or in private, by drinking and exclaiming, "Thy fitness," while at the same time hitting their cups. This is called "Duos" drinking: they are then, "Duus Brodre," (thou brothers) and using the pronoun "thou" to each other ever since, finding it more natural than "De," (you). Parents, sister and brother, you say to each other, regardless of their age or level. Lord and queen claim the Greater to the lesser of their servants. But servants and inferiors don't use the same term for their masters or superiors—nor is it ever used when speaking to a stranger, or someone they're only slightly acquainted with—they then say you, as in English. "I plead your forgiveness," said the wise person; "with me it is an ancient habit. You're absolutely right, and I'm going to remember that; but now you've got to tell me everything you've seen! "That's all! "The shadow said. "For I have seen it all and I believe it all! "How did the furthest saloon look like? "The learned man asked." Was it like in the fresh forest?

Was that like a holy church in there? When we stood on high mountains, were the saloons like the moonlit firmament? ""It was everything! "The shadow said. "I didn't go very in, I waited in the chief room, in the dusk, but I stood there pretty excellently; I saw everything, and I knew everything! I was at Poesy's court in the antechamber.' "So what did you see? Have all of the ancient gods passed through the big saloons? Have the original heroes fought over there? Have sweet kids played there, and related their dreams? "I tell you that I was there, and you will imagine that I saw everything that was to be seen there. You wouldn't have been a man had you come over there; but I became so! And on top of that, I learned to know my inner nature, my innate qualities, the relationship I had with Poesy. I didn't talk of it at the time I was with you, but always — you know it well — when the sun rose, and when the sun had set, I was so oddly great; at the moonlight, I was very close to becoming more distinct than you were; at the moment, I didn't realize my nature; it was explained to me in the anteroom! I just became a kid! I came out mature; but you were no more in the warm territories; I was embarrassed as a man to go as I was. I lacked boots, clothes, and all the human varnish that makes a man perceptible. I've taken my way — I tell you that, but you won't insert it in the book — I've taken my way to the cake lady — I've hid behind her; the lady didn't know so far she's secret. I went out first at night; I ran in the moonlight over the streets; I made myself long up the walls — it tickles my back so delightfully! I ran up and ran down, peeping in the highest windows, in the lounges and on the roofs, and peeping where no one could sneak, I saw what no one else could see, what no one else should see! This is a reference planet too! I wouldn't be a man if it weren't accepted and considered to be something like that now! I saw with the women, with the men, with the mom and dad and with the sweet, matchless children the most unbelievable things; I saw, "said the shadow," what no man must know, but what they would all know so willingly — what is evil in their neighbour. Had I published a newspaper I'd read it! But I wrote directly to the people themselves, and in all the cities I came to, there was consternation. They feared me so much and yet they liked me so extremely. The teachers made me a professor; the tailors gave me new clothes — I'm well furnished; the mint master struck me new coin and the women said I was so beautiful! And so I was the man that I was. And now

I'm biding you farewell. Here's my card — I live on the street's sunshine side, and in rainy season I'm still at home! "And the shadow went so far."That was really extraordinary! "That learnt man said. Years and days passed, and then the shadow returned. "How's it going? "The shadow said. "Woe to me! "The learned man said, 'I write about the true, and the good, and the beautiful, but no one cares to hear such things; I am very desperate, for I take it to heart so much! "But I'm not! "The shadow said. "I 'm getting overweight and it's nobody that needs to be! You don't grasp the world. From that you're going to get sick. You have to go flying! I 'm going to do some tour this summer; are you going to go with me? I want to have a touring companion! Are you going to go with me, like shadow? It's going to be a great pleasure for me to have you with me; I'll pay the costs of traveling! "No, it's too much! "The learned man said, 'It's just like you're taking it! "The shadow said. "Traveling will do you too much harm! Do you want to be my shadow? On the journey you will have everything unrestricted! "Damn, it's too bad! "The learned man said," But with the universe it's just like that! "The shadow said," and that's how it's going to be! "And it went away again. The educated man was by no means in the most enviable state; he was accompanied by sorrow and torture, and what he said about the real and the good and the lovely was, to most people, like roses for a dog! He was in the end very sick. "You look like a shadow, really! "His friends said to him, and the learned man began to shake because he was thinking about it. "Watering-place you must go! "The shadow, who came to see him, said. "For that there is nothing else! For the sake of old friend, I'm going to take you with me; I'm going to pay the traveling expenses, and you're going to write the explanations — and if they're fun for me on the way! I 'm going to a watering place — my beard doesn't grow as it should — that's a sickness as well — and you've got to have a beard! Now you're smart, and take the offer; we're going to fly like comrades! "And so they traveled; the shadow was a master, and the master a shadow; they rode and walked together, side by side, before and after, just as the sun was; the shadow was always careful to keep itself in the place of the master. Now the knowledgeable man didn't think much about it; he was a very kind-hearted man, and particularly gentle and polite, and so one day he said to the shadow: "As we have become partners now, and have grown up together from childhood, are we not to drink 'thou' together, is it more familiar? "You're right," the shadow said, who was the right master now. "It's said in a very direct and well-meaning way. You surely know how weird it is as an educated man. Some people can't bear to touch gray paper, or they get sick; some shiver with every limb if you brush a glass panel with a nail: I just get such a feeling when you hear you tell me; in my first case with you, I feel like I'm pressed to the floor. You see it's a feeling; it's not a feeling of pride: I didn't expect you to tell me THOU, but I willfully say THOU, so it's half done! "So the shadow told their former master THOU. It's pretty bad," he thought, "that I have to say YOU and he's saying THOU," but now he's been forced to stick with it. And they came to a watering-place where many visitors were present, and among them was a princess who was distressed to see too well; and that was so frightening! She clearly noted that the visitor who had just arrived was such a different kind of guy than all the others; "He came here to get his beard to grow, they say, but I see the true reason, he can't cast a shadow." She had become inquisitive; and so she entered into direct conversation with the odd fellow, on their walks. She didn't have to stand on trifles like a king's daughter, so she said, "Your complaint is that you can't cast a shadow? "Your Royal Highness will be significantly strengthened," the shadow said, "I know that your concern is that you see it very plainly, however it has reduced, you are cured. I've just got a really unusual shadow! Do you not see the guy who goes with me all the time? Some people have a shadow in common so I don't like what's normal to everybody. For their livery we give our servants finer cloth than we use ourselves, and so I had my shadow trimmed into a man: yes, you see I even gave him a shadow. It's a little pricey but I enjoy doing it for myself! "What!" "The Princess thought. "I sure should be healed! Those baths are the world's first! Water has powerful forces in our day. Yet I'm not going to abandon the spot because it's starting to be fun here now. I love the stranger so much: wouldn't his beard grow, because in that case he will abandon us! "The princess and the shadow danced in the main ballroom together throughout the evening. She was sweet, but he was smaller still; she had never had such a dance partner. She asked him what kind of land she came from, and he knew the country; he'd been there, but then she wasn't at home; he'd looked in at the window above and below — he'd seen all of them, and he could address the princess, and make insinuations, and she'd been very amazed; he'd be the wisest guy in the universe! She sensed that respect for what he knew! And she fell in love with him as they danced together again; and even the shadow should say, for she almost stabbed him with her lips. So they danced together again; and she was about to assert herself, but she was discreet; she was aware of her land and country, and of the many people she would have to rule. "He's a wise man," she said to herself—"its fine; and he dances delightfully — that's fine as well; but does he have solid knowledge? That is equally important! He must be investigated. "So she began to ask him, by degrees, about the hardest things she could think about, and she couldn't answer them herself; so the shadow made a funny smile. "Unable to answer these questions? "The princess said. "They are part of the learning process in my youth," the shadow said. "I truly believe my shadow can answer them by the door there! ""Thy shadow!" "The princess said. "That would be terrific indeed! "I'm not going to know for sure," the shadow said, "but I assume so; he's been watching me for so many years now and listening to my conversation — I would hope it's likely. Yet your royal highness will allow me to say that he is so proud to pass himself off for a man that he must be handled very like a man when he is to be in a proper mood—and he must be so to respond well." "Oh! I love it! "The princess said. So she went by the door to the wise man and talked to him about the sun and the moon and about people in and out of the world and he replied with wisdom and pragmatism. "What a man he must be to have a shadow so wise! "She thought. "It's going to be a real blessing for my people and the empire if I choose him for my prince — I'm going to! "They were soon agreed, both the princess and the shadow; but before she came into her own kingdom no one should know about it. "No one- not my shadow! "The shadow said, and he had his own ideas! Now when she was at home, they were in the region where the princess reigned. "Listen, my good friend," the shadow said to the learned man. "Now I've become as happy and powerful as anybody can be; so I'll do something special for you! You shall always live with me in the castle, drive with me in my royal carriage, and have ten thousand pounds a year; but then you shall be called SHADOW by all and by all; you shall not say that you have ever been a man; and once a year you shall lie at my feet as a shadow do! I have to tell you: I'm going to marry the daughter of the king and the nuptials are going to take place tonight! "No, it's going too far! "The learned man said, 'I am not going to have it; I am not going to! To trick the nation as a whole and the princess too! I'll tell you all! That I'm a man, and you're a shadow, you're dressed up! "No one is going to believe it! "The shadow said. "Be fair or I'll call the watchman! "I 'm going to the princess immediately! "The learned man said, 'But, I'm going to go first! "The shadow said. "And you go to prison! "And he needed to do that — for the sentinels obeyed him because they knew the daughter of the king was to marry. "You're just shaking! "When the shadow came into her chamber, the princess said. "Would something have happened? You don't have to be unwell this evening, now that we're going to be celebrating our nuptials." "I've lived to see the cruelest thing anyone can live to see! "The shadow said. "Think just — yes, it's real, such a bad shadow-skull can't take much — think just, my shadow has gone mad; imagine he's a man, and I — now just believe — that I am his shadow! "What a horrible thing! "The princess said; but he's confined, isn't he? "That's it. I fear he will never recover." "Poor shadow! "The princess said. "He's very unfortunate; it would be a real work of charity to deliver him from the little life he's got, and when I think about it properly, I think it's going to be necessary to quietly do away with him! "Surely it is difficult," the shadow said, "For he was a faithful servant! "And he gave a sort of sigh then. "You're a noble person! "The princess said. In the evening, the entire city was illuminated, and the cannons left with a bum! Bum! Fuck you! And the troops turned up weapons. What a life it was! Princess and shadow went out to show themselves on the balcony, and get another hurrah! The learned man heard nothing of all this — for he had been deprived of life by them.

Chapter 2: Bed Time Fictional Stories

In this Chapter some wonderful fictional stories have been added read and enjoy

2.1 The Covetous Aristocrats

Once a very popular artist who resided in Eindhoven, a small town. He produced such outstanding work that the Elector, Prince Rolland, commissioned a bronze sculpture image of itself, on horseback. The artist was elated at the Committee, then worked at the site late & early. The job was eventually finished, and the architect got the magnificent monument put in place on Eindhoven's town square, prepared for the sight to launch. The super delegate was arriving on the designated day and his closest nobles were arriving from the castle alongside him. Then, it revealed the monument. This was very stunning, — so magnificent that the heir to the throne in shock gasped. He couldn't look enough so, like an old buddy, he walked to the artist then shook hands with him. "Ross Pedro," he stated, 'you are a brilliant artist, and this sculpture will push your reputation much higher than already is; a fantastic image of me! 'When the nobles realized this, and saw the gentle hand hold, their architect's indignation is out control. Their one idea was, what they can easily do anything to embarrass him. They won't dare to find faults in the photo sculpture, for the prince had pronounced it flawless, but after that one of them said, with such an air of utter boldness, "Ah, Ross Pedro, the image of his majesty is perfect. But let me admit that the horse's sculpture might not be as efficient: the head is too big; out of ratio. "No," another added, 'the horse's not actually that perfect; the turn of neck is not perfect, there, is awkward. "If you were to adjust the right hind foot, Ross Pedro," a third stated, "that would be an upgrade'." Another flaw with the horse's snout also discovered. Silently the performer heard. While they had all done, he returned to the prince and then said, "Your nobles, Lord, find a fair number of faults in the horse's sculpture; would you allow me to hold it an another few days, to do just what I could about it? The Elector gave his consent, and the designer had a provisional shield installed across the model, so his subordinates may perform without interference.

The sound of thumping came out continuously from behind wall for many days. The aristocrats, who always took precautions to travel that way, were pleased. -- one said to itself, "I really must've been correct; the maker himself sees something inaccurate; Now I will have credit for my aesthetic appeal for rescuing the prince's depiction!

"The artist once again called the prince and his nobles, and the statue was revealed once again. The Prince once more bellowed at his magnificence, and then ended up turning to his aristocrats to see what they'd have to say, one after the other. "Well-done!' "First said. "Now that the head of the horse is proportionate, there's no mistake."" "The adjustment in the collar was exactly what it took," the second said; "it is really gracious now. "The right back foot is how it should be now," third wrote, "and it brings so much to the entire elegance! "The fourth claimed he found the tail to have changed tremendously. "My nobles are happy now," the prince told Ross Pedro; "they find the sculpture has changed a lot with the improvements you developed."

Ross Pedro chuckled a bit. "I'd love that they're satisfied," he added, "but the truth is, I didn't adjust anything! "What do you say?" the prince asked "Didn't we hear the pummeling noise each day? What were you trying to hammer at that time?" "I was hammering at the courtiers' image, who find blame only as they are greedy," the designer said. "And I feel their image is fairly much pounded into bits! "It was, really. The Elector grinned wholeheartedly, though without warning the nobles were slumping down, one by one.

2.2 Rebecca of Toronto

If you've been to the wonderful city of Toronto, someone will surely take you down to the old industry section of the city, where banks are headquartered and stores and restaurants, and you'll see a statute on the road. It is the sculpture of a lady sitting in a low seat, leaning against her and the her arms across a child. The woman isn't beautiful whatsoever: she's wearing heavy, typical boots, a simple top, a little quilt and a solar-bonnet; she's sturdy and thin, and her face is a square-chinned Irish one; yet her eyes look like your mom's. But there's something really interesting about all this monument: that's the first one ever created in a female's commemoration in this state. There aren't many statues to women including in old Europe, most of the few are to wonderful princesses and queens, very young and very lushly attired. You see, this monument is not quite like everything else in Toronto.

This is a depiction of Rebecca. Her full identity was Rebecca Thompson but by that nobody in Toronto knows her, no more than you think of her full name as your dearly beloved sister; she is just Rebecca. That's her origin and it explains that why people made her a symbol.

When Rebecca was a small kid, her mom and dad passed, and two young people raised her as poor and as loving as their own family. She stayed with them prior until growing up. She later married, then and has her own little boy. But her husband died very early and afterwards the infant also died and Rebecca was all alone in universe. She was weak but solid and she learned how to handle. She ironed dresses in a laundry the whole day, from dawn to dusk. And as she started working by the window each day, she noticed a small motherless kids coming from the orphan asylum, close by, and constantly playing around. A great illness fell upon the city for a while, yet so many moms and dads perished that there were more survivors than asylum could actually provide for.

Now, they wanted a decent buddy. You too would imagine, would you that even a poor girl who was working in a laundry might be a friend to each other? Still, it was Rebecca. She went directly to the compassionate nuns who had the asylum and informed them she would give them some of her wages and go Other than, to work with them. She had worked incredibly hard very long that she had saved a lot of money from the salaries. With this she purchased two cows and a small cart for distribution. Instead, every dawn, she took her milk to her buyers in the little cart; and as she passed, she pleaded the left-over food from the hotels and wealthy homes, and put it back into the cart to the asylum starving kids. In the most stressful moments that was also all the nutrition that the kids got.

A portion of the money Rebecca received went to the asylum each week, and after a number of years it was even greater and stronger. And Rebecca was so cautious and good at trade that she purchased many cows and gained extra profit, while offering them. She established a home for newborn kids with this; she named it her kid home. Rebecca had an opportunity to get a cake shop after a period and then she was a bread-woman rather than a dairy-woman. She put the bread in her basket, just as she had brought the food. And yet she kept offering asylum cash. Then there is our war came as a big battle. Rebecca decided to drive her cart of bread in all the distress and illness and dread of that moment; and then somehow, except what she sold, she every time would have enough to give to the hungry troops, and for her babies. And amidst all this she earned enough just to build a large steam manufacturing plant for her bread when the conflict was over.

By that same time she was familiar to everyone in the area. The kids in the town loved her; the merchants were respectful of her; even the poor families came to her for help. She used to sit in a calico dress and a little silk scarf, at the open front door of her office, and give all, rich or poor, a better term. But one day, by and large, Rebecca has died. But when it was necessary to publish her will, the citizens learned that she had already saved a considerable amount of money for all her donating, and how she had donated every penny of it to the city's various orphan asylums, —every one of them got everything. Either for white and black kids, Jews, Catholics or Protestants, it won't make any difference; Rebecca always said, "They all are all survivor sand just remember, precious ones, the lovely, wiser will was marked with across rather than a signature, since Rebecca never learned how to write & read!

When the people of Toronto knew Rebecca was deceased, they stated ", "She was a mother to the parentless; she was a companion to those who had no acquaintances; she had more intellect than educational institutions can instruct; human's not going to let her remembrance get beyond us." So they decided to make a monument of her, just but she used to look, seated in her own office door or going to drive in her own little cart.

2.3 The Dress-Maker and the Three Behemoths

Once upon a time there was a Dress-Maker in Galway, and he set out on a trip and go to the Sussex grand jury of the Queen. He hadn't traveled far until he saw a winged horse and he praised him. "God bless you" the Dress-Maker said. "God bless you" the horse said. "Where do you go?"' "I 'm moving to London," the Dress-Maker said, "Building a court for the lord and getting a woman for a wife, if I can do it." Indeed, it seems that the king had given his princess and a huge amount of money to anybody who can construct his court. The problem was that three goliaths resided by the court in the forest, and they emerged out of the forest at night, and ripped down everything that was constructed by day. So, no one was really willing to build the court. "Will you give me a hole," said the white old horse, "where I might go hide if the crowd were to carry me to the farm or even to the furnace, so that they'd not see me, because they had lost me to do their job." "I would certainly do that, "the Dress-Maker replied, "and accept. "He managed to bring his pickaxe and plow, and he drilled a hole, and told the white old stallion to go away quickly into it, until he saw if it fitted him. The white horse fell into the gap, although he was unable to rise out again as he attempted to. "Create a spot for me anyway," the white horse stated, "with when I get thirsty, I'll show back out of the hollow here." "I'm not going to," said the Dress-Maker;' sit wherever you are before I get back, and I'm going to pick you up."

The next day when the Dress-Maker stepped forward, and the fox encountered him. 'God protect thee,' the fox said. "God protect you!" The Dress-Maker replied. "Where would you travel," the fox asked." I 'm going to Sussex to compete, I'm expecting to be able to reach the King's court. "Can you create a place to hide for me?" asked the fox. "The majority of the foxes attack me, so they don't let me do something like them. "I'm going to do it for you"' the Dress-Maker said. He held his axe and saw, then created a box, then advised the fox to move into it before he saw how it would suit him. The fox got into it, so once the Dress-Maker had him down, he locked him in. Once the fox was eventually pleased that he had a comfortable position inside, he begged the Dress-Maker to let himself out, and then the Dress-Maker responded that he would not. "Wait before I get back there again," he states.

The Dress-Maker went ahead the very next day, and when he reached a place he had not gone too far; and he was welcomed by the lion. "God help you', 'the lion said." God help you!" the Dress-Maker replied. Where do you go?"' the lion asked.

"I 'm going to Sussex before I can reach the emperor's court, if I can do it," the Dress-Maker stated. "Then you'd have to construct a plough for me," the lion replied, "I as well as the other lions will be plowing and scrambling since we had enough to eat from the crop. "I'm going to do it for you"' the Dress-Maker said.

He took his hammer and his eye, and constructed a plough. After the plough was built, he put holes in the beam of it, and said to the lion that he would go under the plow until he knew that it was perfect for a ploughman. He put the tail of the lion throughout the hole he had created for it, and then hollered it in a frame, so the lion could not pull his tail anymore. "Quickly lose me now," the lion stated, "and we're going to patch everything, start trudging."

The Dress-Maker said he'd never let him back He abandoned him, and returned to Sussex, before he got back himself. As he arrived in Sussex, he had construction workers and started to create the building. By the end of each day, he let the staff place a huge rock on top of working. Once the big stone was lifted, the Dress-Maker place a sort of obstinacy under it, so that he could bring it back as quickly as the behemoth reached as close as it was.

As the dark of the night arrived, he saw three behemoths coming, and they started to throw down the courtyard till they arrived as far as the spot where the Dress-Maker was hidden up above, and a man of them hit his sledge at the spot where he had been. The Dress-Maker started throwing the stone, and it dropped on him and destroyed him.

The tradesmen came the very next day again and operated until night and the Dress-Maker went home He told them to put the big boulder on top of the project, like it was the night prior. They accomplished it for him, they headed off, and the Dress-Maker returned to hide the same thing that he had done the night previously.

When the citizens had gone to bed, the two behemoths appeared and started throwing everything that was around them, and as long as they began, they sent out two yells from them. The Dress-Maker kept on maneuvering till he flung down the massive stone, and it dropped on the behemoths 's head that was beneath him, and it destroyed him. Then there's only the one behemoth left in it, yet he never returned back until the court was constructed.

However when the job was completed, the Dress-Maker returned to the emperor and asked him to offer him his spouse and his property, because he had done the court; and the emperor said he might not offer him any spouse unless he destroyed the other behemoth, for he said he'd never destroyed the 2 behemoths by his power before any of this, and that he'd owe him hardly anything before he destroyed other for him.

Happy to contribute; there's no pause on that at all. Then the Dress-Maker returned to the spot in which the other behemoths was, and questioned if he wanted steward-boy. The behemoth replied he wanted one, because he could find one which would do whatever he may do instead. "Whatever you choose, I'll do this," the Dress-Maker replied.

So they proceeded to their supper, and once they had consumed it, the behemoth told the Dress-Maker, "Perhaps it comes with him just to consume quite enough soup as him, out from its brewing." The Dress-Maker replied, "This will arrive with me to do just that, but you should offer me an hour until we start on it." Then the Dress-Maker headed out, and he found a lamb hide, and he stitched it up and once he produced a sack of it, then went back.

The Dress-Maker let drop a quart to the skin, but the behemoth figured he'd drink it. "I'm trying to go for it and it isn't starting to appear for you to do something," the Dress-Maker stated. "You won't," the behemoths replied. "What would you do?" "Take a crack, and let the liquid out yet again," the Dress-Maker stated. "Try this yourself first," the behemoth added. The Dress-Maker offered a knife poke, and he let out the broth from the fur. "Do this you'," he said." I would," the behemoth stated, bringing such a knife jab out of his own gut that he slaughtered himself. That's how the Dress-Maker assassinated the third behemoth.

So he returned to the emperor and requested him to give his spouse and wealth to him, so that he'd throw the court down once until he had the woman. So they were terrified he might thrown the court down, so they sent the bride to him. Just after Dress-Maker had gone a day, the people after him expressed remorse and pursued him to take his wife home again. They returned to the spot wherever the lion was, so the lion spoke to them, 'Yesterday the Dress-Maker and his spouse were here. I saw them walking by, and if you lose me now, I am quicker than you, and I will chase them till I overpower them.' When they learned that, they loosed the lion out.

The lion and the citizens of Sussex moved on, and they followed him before they got to the spot wherever the fox was, and the fox addressed them, saying, 'This afternoon the Dress-Maker and his spouse were here, so if you lose me out, I'm faster than you, so I'm going to chase them and capture them. 'So the lion and the fox and the Sussex soldier moved on, attempting to capture the Dress-Maker, and they moved to the spot where the elderly white horse was, and the old Whitehorse revealed to everyone that the Dress-Maker and his companion were here in the morning, and he stated, 'Let me out,' he added, 'I'm quicker than you, and I'm going to ambush them.'

The Dress-Maker and his wife were pursued by Sussex army and the fox, lion and horse alongside, and it was not long until they met up with him, until they saw him and his wife.

Once the Dress-Maker spotted them approaching, he and his wife stepped out of the coach and sat quietly on the ground. Once the elderly white horse saw Dress-Maker lying on the field, he stated, "That's the position he had before he created the pit for me, I couldn't get out of it when I fell down into it. I'm not going to go any closer to it." "No!" the fox responded, "Because that's the way he was doing it for me, so I'm not going to get any closer to him. "No!" the lion says, "Because that's how it was when he made the plowing which I was trapped. I'm not going to get any closer to him. "They all went back from him anyway, and arrived home to Galway with his princess.

2.4 The Fortress of Luck

One glorious sunny morning, even as the sun was rising, passengers set off on a trip. Both of them were solid young men but one was a slow guy and the other a worker. When the first sun rays rolled over the mountains, they reflected as far ahead as the eye might reach, on a huge building built on the peaks. This was a magnificent and majestic building, with the gleaming towers gleaming like stone, and looking directly openings sparkling like ice. The 2 guys enthusiastically gazed at it, and aspired to get near.

Unexpectedly something more like a huge butterfly, of gold and white, flew at them from the range. And as it got closer, they could see it was a very stunning girl, robed as fine as twigs in spinning clothes and carrying a crown so brilliant on her forehead no one could tell if it was gem or dew. She remained silent, soft as wind, on a tall, bright, golden ball that rolls with it, faster than the sea. She turned her attention to them as she approached the passengers, and grinned. "Follow me on! "She told. The idle man sat up in the field with an uncomfortable face. "She's had a great way! "Did he say? But the laborious man rushed after the stunning woman and grabbed the fringe in his grip of her spinning dress. "Who really are you and where do you go? "Questioned. "I am just the Luck Fairy," further said pretty woman, "but that is my palace. If you like, you can hit it now; there's time, if you don't lose it. If you approach it before midnight's last part, I'll get you somewhere, and be your buddy. Even if you come past midnight for a second, it would be very late."' The robe slid off the foreigner's hand until she had just said and she was disappeared. Immediately rushed to his mate, the laborious man asked him whatever the fairy had meant. "Idea!' "the stupid man said, and he giggled;' obviously, if a pony had a body There'd be a possibility to walk that route all the way? No, no. Please. " "So take care," his companion stated, "I 'm going." And he started off with a strong reasonable pace, his head directly ahead, down a path towards the sparkling fortress.

The lazy man laid in the wet grass, and gazed at the distant land towers quite dreamily. "If I had just a decent pony, oh!" he gasped. He started to feel stuff warm at his shoulder at that point of time, and got to hear that little shrill. He started to turn round, yet there stepped a little stallion! It was a delicate animal, smooth-looking, and delicately built, saddled and sneered.

"Heyyyy!" "Luck always arrives when someone is 'not seeking for it!'" stated the lazy man. "And in another moment he jumped up on the pony and headed for the luck castle. The tiny animal proceeded at a perfect pace, and within a few moments they overtook the second traveler, moving on foot.

"How would you like a horse maul? "The lazy man smiled, as his companion walked by. The laborious man just shrugged and held eyes directly ahead with his continuous movement. The pony kept its fast speed, and by midday the fortress pillars shone out against the horizon, far closer and more majestic. Precisely at midday, the animal moved to a dark meadow on a hill aside from the road and halted.

"Wise beast," stated his rider;' "hasty causes waste,' and in moderation, all becomes easier. I'm trying to pursue your lead, and eat or rest a little. "He jumped down and sat quietly against a pine in the cold grass. He was having a snack from the pocket of his traveler bag and he enjoyed it happily. Soon from the sun and early trip he felt dizzy, putting his cap over his head and calming down to sleep. "A little rest is going to go all the way," he added.

It was a nightmare! He was sleeping like the 7 sleepers, and dreaming of the most incredible places you can picture. Eventually, he dreamed of reaching the fortress of luck and being greeted with fantastic celebrations. What he'd like was He was taken to him, and band playing in his recognition as flares were fired off. The song had become so intense he awakened. He stood up and opened his eyes, and indeed, the very last beams of the sun setting are its flares, and the rhythm was the other tourist's words, crossing the meadow on feet!

"Time to get gone," the lazy person stated, and reached for the beautiful horse around him. No pony was located. Aged, bony, greyish donkey was really the only living creature nearby. The chap called, and shouted, and gazed, but there was no small horse. He gave it up after a long spell, and because there was little else to do, he rode the donkey and started off again.

The donkey was difficult and slow to handle although he was greater than none at all; and the lazy person slowly saw the walls of the fortress draw closer.

Now it started to grow dark; the lights started to appear in the castle windows. Then trouble came! The greyish donkey moved weaker and weaker; slower and slower, until he halted and stayed still in the very center of a ball-black forest. Not a single move

He is swinging with all the cajoling and chiding that his driver might offer. The driver kicked him and also hit him, and the donkey thought he have plenty on that. His back legs-heels did go up, and his face came down, and the poor guy went off to the craggy surface. He laid there grumbling for several moments, and we can tell you it wasn't a comfortable spot. How he wishes he was in a safe, comfy house, in sheets relaxed with his achy joints! The mere sight of it caused him recall the luck palace, for he figured good beds must have been there. He was still able to bestir his fractured bones to get into these sheets and he stood up and cared for the donkey around him.

No donkey has been found. The lazy person scraped his hands on the middle stump, ripped his facial features in the brambles, and popped his legs into the rocks. While there was no donkey. He should have languished back once more to sleep, but he was now able to hear the yelps of rabid dogs in the forest; that won't look good.

Eventually, his palm grasped something This one felt like a sling. Happily, he recognized it, and began to climb his donkey. The creature he took care of appeared to be very small, and as he climbed he felt its sides wet and slimy. This gave him a chill and he reluctant; then he noticed a remote bell click at that time. It hit eleven! There's already time to get to the luck palace, but not more than sufficient; so he rode his new steed and sat on it once again. The animal was harder to balance on than the donkey, and the seat appeared to be surprisingly high apart; leaning against felt fine. Although the donkey wasn't quite as sluggish as this; the new steed was quicker than he was. Even so, after a moment, he worked his escape out from the forest into the country, and the fortress stood there, only a little way away! Both the windows were lights alight. A light from them dropped upon the creature of the lazy person, and he saw whatever he was riding: a giant snail! A snail the equivalent of a horse!

A freezing trembling passed through the lazy guy's body, and there and then he'd get off his wretched pig, but only then the Timer hit again. This was one of the first long, slow midnight movements to mark! Once he realized that, the man was anxious. He pounded his feet into the sides of the snail, to rush him. The snail immediately drew in his face, snuggled in his shell, and left the poor person lying on the floor in a pile! The timer hit twice. He still could have managed to reach the castle if the man would have run for it, but rather, he sat very still hollered for a horse. "A beast, you beast!' "He cried, 'some sort of creature that leads me to the palace!" The clock hit 3 times. And as it hit the third reference, stuff came clattering and whirring out of the shadows, something which actually sounds like a tethered horse. A very Trans gendered, low back, the lazy guy jumped on his back. As he positioned, he saw fortress doors wide open, and he saw his buddy stepping on the cutoff, flashing his cap and nudging at him.

The bell hit 4 times, and the new stallion started to stir; he pushed a step forward as it hit five; he halted when it hit six; he did strike seven, Turned around; when it reached eight, he started moving backwards, away from the palace! The poor man screamed and hit him, but the brute slowly turned around. So the clock hit nine. Then the guy tried to slide down, but on both directions of his peculiar animal huge arms rose out and kept him tight. And then in the next ray of light of the moon that split the black shadows, he realized that he was placed on a crab with monsters! The lamps went out at once, in the doors of the fortress. The clock hit ten. The crab lost momentum. Twice! The crab then moved backwards. The clock hit 12! And the big doors closed with a clacking, and the luck fortress was locked the lazy person probably forever.

No-one knows exactly what happened of him and his crab to this very day, and no-one minds. But the hardworking man was welcomed by the Luck Fairy and cheered up in the fortress as much as he wished to live. Ever since, she remained his companion, not just encouraging him to be content with himself, but also teaching him how to support others everywhere he went'

CPSIA information can be obtained
at www.ICGtesting.com
Printed in the USA
LVHW050342210621
690733LV00003B/223